Desert

LONDON, NEW YORK,
MELBOURNE, MUNICH, and DELHI

Written and edited by Fleur Star
Designed by Clare Shedden

Publishing manager Susan Leonard
Managing art editor Rachael Foster
Picture researcher Liz Moore
Production Sarah Jenkins
DTP designer Ben Hung
Jacket designer Mary Sandberg

Consultant Dr Kim Dennis-Bryan

First published in Great Britain in 2007 by
Dorling Kindersley Limited
80 Strand, London WC2R 0RL

Copyright © 2007 Dorling Kindersley Limited
A Penguin Company

2 4 6 8 10 9 7 5 3 1
ED506 – 05/07

A CIP catalogue record for this book
is available from the British Library.

ISBN 978-1-40531-885-3

Colour reproduction by Colourscan, Singapore
Printed and bound in Italy by L.E.G.O.

Discover more at
www.dk.com

Contents

4-5
What is a desert?

6-7
Where in the world?

8-9
Stacks of sand

10-11
Dust storm!

12-13
Water of life

14-15
The Sahara

16-17
Staying alive

18-19
Night hunters

20-21
Poison!

22-23
Camels up close

24-25
Down under

26-27
Cactus country

28-29
The desert in bloom

30-31
Who lives there?

32-33
Desert daily life

34-35
Food and drink

36-37
Twice as tough

38-39
Living in the Gobi

40-41
It's cool to be coastal

42-43
Is it a desert?

44-45
The growing desert

46-47
Glossary

48
Index and
acknowledgements

What is a desert?

About one-fifth of the world is desert – arid (dry) land where less than 25 cm (10 in) of rain falls in a whole year. Most people think that deserts are hot, sandy, empty places – but is that true for every desert?

"Deserts are just a load of sand."
Sandy deserts, such as the Sahara, may have huge sand dunes, but they are mostly made up of rocks and gravel. Many desert have oases or rivers flowing through them

Cactus plants grow in American deserts, such as the Sonoran.

Camels easily cross the large dunes in the Sahara Desert.

"There's no life in the desert."

Compared to other parts of the world, such as forests, deserts are quite empty. But there are plants, animals, and even people living in deserts.

"It's hot in the desert."

Not always! Coastal deserts are cool, and cold deserts have freezing days during the winter. Even in hot deserts, where the Sun beats down during the day, it gets very cold at night.

The Atacama Desert is cool because it is high up in the mountains.

Where in the world?

There are different ways of describing a desert, such as by temperature (is it hot or cold?) or where it is (is it on the coast?). Most deserts are near the tropics, where the weather is hot and dry.

Which is the only continen

Map key

● Hot deserts – these are very hot during the day, and any water here evaporates quickly.

● Cool coastal deserts – these deserts have cool air blowing in from the sea.

● Cold deserts – these have extremely cold winters, but they can still be very hot in the summer.

● Antarctic – this desert is unlike any other: it's frozen!

NORTH AMERICA

Great Basin

Sonoran

Tropic of Cancer   Mojave

Chihuahua

Equator

SOUTH AMERICA

Atacama

Tropic of Capricorn

Patagonia

Hot deserts are subtropical: they lie near the tropics of Cancer and Capricorn. This is the hottest part of the globe.

Coastal deserts are also subtropical, but they are not as warm as hot deserts because cold currents in the ocean keep the air cool.

Europe

Cold deserts lie outside the tropics, further away from the equator than hot deserts. A band of cold deserts stretches across central Asia.

...hat doesn't have a desert?

EUROPE

Kara Kum   Kyzyl Kum
                      Gobi
            Takla Makan

Great Salt Desert   ASIA

MIDDLE EAST

Sahara   Thar

        Arabian

AFRICA

Namib
        Kalahari

Great Sandy   Tanami

Gibson   Simpson

Great Victoria   AUSTRALIA

ANTARCTICA

Antarctica is not like other deserts because it never gets hot. There's no water here because the snow doesn't melt.

Answer:

7

Stacks of sand

Deserts aren't entirely made up of sand – many of them are full of rocks and gravel too. But there are still thousands of square kilometres (miles) of sand. So where did it all come from?

Elephant Rock is in the Mojave Desert, USA.

Elephants rock!

As mountains wear away, they leave behind shapes called pinnacles. Many look like towers or needles, but others appear as arches or even animals.

Wind also creates sand, blowing across sandstone mountains and reducing them to dust.

From mighty mountains...

Most of the tiny grains of sand found in sandy deserts were once mountains! They were worn down by ice and water that covered the planet millions of years ago.

It can take hundreds of years for the wind to carve through the huge rocks.

Funny flowers

Desert roses are not real plants, but are made of crystals. When groundwater evaporates, it leaves behind crystals. These grow between grains of sand, creating "flowers".

Colourful carvings

These amazing rocks have been carved into shape by the wind. As the outer layers wear away, it reveals the colourful layers – or strata – of different types of rock that make up the mountains.

The world's highest dune is in the Gobi.
It is around 500 m (1,640 ft) tall.

Dazzling dunes
Dunes are big hills of
sand that are blown into
shape by the wind. Plants
or other obstacles block
the sand and stop it
moving, so it piles up
into a dune.

*Dunes can form different
shapes, depending on the
direction the wind blows.
This one, in the Namib
Desert, is crescent shaped.*

Dust storm!

A solid-looking wall of dust 1.5 km (1 mile) high is coming towards you. Suddenly the air is thick with swirling dust; it gets into your clothes and possessions, you can't see, and you can't breathe. Watch out, it's a dust storm!

Caught out

While robes and veils keep out the worst of the storm, dust still gets inside clothes. The only thing to do if caught outside in a storm is to huddle together and wait it out.

Saving face

Camels are too big to hide from a storm, but they can close their nostrils to stop sand getting up their noses. A thin third eyelid brushes sand out of their eyes.

Long eyelashes stop much of the sand getting into the eyes.

Stormy city
Beijing, in China, is more than 1,600 km (1,000 miles) from the Gobi Desert. But six times a year, Gobi dust turns the city's air yellow, making it difficult to breathe.

What are dust storms?
They are strong winds that blow huge gusts of dust for thousands of kilometres (miles). The dust is made of sand that the weather has worn into fine grains.

You devil!
Dust devils are common in desert areas where the land is flat and the air is still. In America these whirling winds that pick up dust are called "dancing devils"; in Australia they are "willy willies".

SINGING DUNES
A Saharan legend tells the story of spirits, or *djenouns*, that sing from inside sand dunes. What really happens is that, in the evening after a storm, the wind causes sand grains to slip down the dune. The moving sand makes a deep groaning sound – the dune is singing!

Storms can be made up of both dust and sand.

The stronger the wind, the further the dust will be blown.

Sand is too heavy to be blown far. It can be lifted 50 cm (2 ft) above ground.

Water of life

An oasis is a source of life in the dry desert. Plants grow where underground water is close to the surface; animals come to drink from the pools; and nomads move their homes to be near the water.

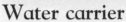

Water carrier

Sandgrouse really fill up at an oasis! They soak up water in their breast feathers, and then fly back to their nests so their chicks can drink it.

Dried dates

Dates are a staple food for people in the desert. There may be 1,000 dates in each huge bunch. Once dried, the fruit will never rot.

Date palms are typically found in North Africa and the Middle East.

Water fall

The water in an oasis comes from rainfall – but it might not have fallen here. Water can seep through porous rocks underground and come to the surface where the ground is low.

Thirsty work

Sometimes water in a desert needs a little help in coming to the surface. These people from a village in the Sahara draw their water from a well they have dug.

River Nile, Africa

Going green

Some deserts have rivers running through them. The water is useful for irrigation: turning barren sand into fertile farmland.

Safety in numbers

Many animals gather at oases, so it's wise to keep a look out for predators while drinking. This pair of gemsbok take turns to drink and stand guard.

Providing for the family

Twice a day, women in the Thar Desert, India, walk many kilometres (miles) to fill their pots with water. They carry the heavy loads home on their heads.

13

The Sahara

The world's biggest desert covers almost the entire north of Africa. The Sahara is a hot desert, which means it is hot during the day all year round: the temperature can reach 58 °C (136 °F) on a summer's day.

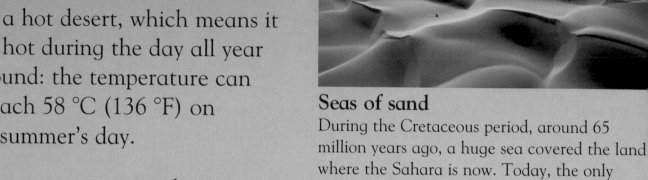

Seas of sand

During the Cretaceous period, around 65 million years ago, a huge sea covered the land where the Sahara is now. Today, the only "seas" in Africa are those made up of sand.

The Arabic word *sahra* gives the Sahara its name. It means "desert".

The real Sahara

Imagine a typical Sahara view: huge *ergs*, or sand dunes, as far as the eye can see... Actually, the Sahara is only 15 per cent sand. Most of the rest is made up of gravel or rock, called *reg* and *hammada*.

Sensible sunbathing
Cold-blooded rainbow lizards warm up in the morning sunshine, becoming bright blue and red as they get hotter. When the sun gets too strong, they shelter under rocks to avoid being cooked.

Locust overload
There are more insects in the desert than any other animal. Just one swarm of locusts may contain millions of the plant-eating pests. They strip plants in minutes, leaving nothing for anything else to eat.

Find out about me on page 22!

Dromedary camels live in the Sahara, but they are not wild.

Staying alive

Deserts are dry places where water and food are in short supply. Animals out searching for food during the day also have to cope with the extreme heat in hot deserts. So how do the animals survive?

The toad burrows backwards, pushing away sand with its spade-like feet.

Who needs to drink?
A spadefoot toad can stay under-ground for months. It wraps itself in a cocoon of dried skin and lives off the water stored in its bladder.

Food and drink
Many small antelopes, such as these springbok, graze on grasses and leaves. They get enough water to survive just from their food – but given the chance they will also drink from pools.

When the feet on the ground get too hot, the lizard changes over.

Cool moves
Shovel snouted lizards keep cool by dancing! They lift up their feet two at a time to avoid burning them on the hot desert floor.

We've got it licked

Red kangaroos lick their forearms to beat the heat: when the saliva evaporates, it cools them down. They can also smell out water, and will travel 200 km (125 miles) to find water during drought.

STOCKING UP

Camels survive in the desert through storing food – not by burying a stash, but by eating when they can and converting the food into fat, which the camel stores in its hump. Some other animals share this survival tip: both fat-tailed gerbils and Gila monsters (a species of lizard) store food in their tails.

Sidewinding snake species include some vipers and adders.

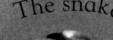

The snake curls up to make a loop, lifts the loop off the sand, and throws it forward to move along.

Making tracks

Sidewinder snakes don't slither forwards, but travel sideways in an S-shape. This way, only part of the snake's belly comes in contact with the hot sand.

The tracks show where the snake lifts up and sets down.

Taking a dive

Sand skinks are also called sandfish because they "swim" through the sand. The sand is a little cooler just beneath the surface, and it's also a safe place to hide.

Night hunters

Even in hot deserts, temperatures plummet at night because there are no clouds in the sky to keep in the heat. Animals that find the daytime too hot come out at sunset, ready to find food.

Sharp eyes

Owls are expert night-time hunters. Their large eyes allow lots of light to pass through, and they also have excellent hearing. Loose feathers on the owl's wings help it fly silently.

The cute-looking cat is really a sharp-clawed, big-toothed, fearsome predator.

Sand cats are about the same size as a small pet cat, but have much thicker fur.

Night facts

- Many animals that are nocturnal (active at night), such as foxes, have thick fur to keep them warm. During the day, the fur reflects the sun.

- Rodents are too small to be active in the daytime: they would overheat very quickly.

The viper bares its fangs and strikes at the sand cat in defence.

"Cat"-ch me if you can

Sand cats creep up close to their prey before making a sudden kill with their strong claws and teeth. If there's nothing on the surface to eat, the cat will dig underground.

Scorpions use their tails to inject attackers with venom.

Rodents are eaten by many predators, such as owls, cats, foxes, and snakes.

Little leaper

Jerboas are small rodents, but they take great leaps to escape predators! Bounding across the desert on its powerful hind legs, it races to get to its burrow before an owl grabs it.

I hear you

Hunting in the dark, fennec foxes use their senses of smell and hearing to find food such as insects, which is one reason why they have huge ears.

A sting at both ends

Scorpions have needle-sharp tails packed with venom, but they only use their sting in defence. When hunting for food, such as geckos, they catch prey with their claws.

The agama must kill the scorpion quickly to avoid being stung.

Hunter becomes hunted

The desert agama is a diurnal (daytime) animal that eats small animals. Hunting prey that sleeps during the day makes catching it that much easier!

Poison!

These creatures are among the deadliest in the desert. Whether they have eight legs or none at all, you had better watch your step to avoid them – they may use their venom for attack as well as defence.

Yellow scorpion

Arachnid facts

Scorpions and spiders are both arachnids, and they share a common way of finding food.

● Hunting at night, they feel for vibrations as prey approaches.

● They can feed only on liquids. Once they have killed their prey, they squirt digestive juices all over the victim, turning it into pulp.

Tarantula trap

Rather than spin webs, tarantulas ambush prey. Large tarantulas crush their prey with their huge fangs, but smaller ones kill by biting their victims and injecting venom.

The lizard's tail is its food store. It is full of fat, similar to a camel's hump.

Like all reptiles, the Gila monster has scaly skin. It also has strong legs for digging burrows.

It's a monster

There are just two species of venomous lizards, and the slow-moving, chunky Gila monster is one. It uses its venom to kill small mammals, food that it finds by smell.

Dicing with death

A red and yellow death adder lies camouflaged on the Australian desert floor. The snake waits for prey to cross its path – then makes a surprise strike.

Watching, waiting

The horned viper doesn't rely on just camouflage. It buries itself in the sand, with just its eyes and horns showing, and lies in wait for its prey.

Snake, rattle, and roll

When a western diamondback rattlesnake is threatened, it coils up and shakes its rattle in defence. But while the snake is venomous, the rattle is actually harmless.

The rattle is made up of a chain of scales that make a noise when the snake shakes its tail.

The rattlesnake kills by biting its victim and injecting it with venom.

Camels up close

There are two camel species, dromedary and bactrian, but 90 per cent of the world's camels are dromedary. Known as "ships of the desert", camels can carry heavy loads over vast distances.

The camel's top lip is split so it can eat thorny plants.

Many dromedaries live in the Sahara

Extra-long eyelashes protect the camel's eyes from sand.

Camel trains carry people, nomads' tents, or goods to sell at market.

Pale fur reflects the sunlight.

Bactrian brother
The bactrian has two humps, and a thick winter coat that moults in the summer. Many domestic bactrians live in the Gobi Desert, but they are endangered in the wild.

Got the hump

A dromedary has just the one hump, but it can weigh up to 14 kg (30 lb). It contains fat, but when the camel uses up this store of food, the hump flops over to one side.

Thick fur keeps the camel warm at night, and protects against the sun in the day.

...ut there are none left in the wild.

A camel spreads its weight onto large, padded feet that don't sink into the sand when it walks.

Colourful camels

People decorate their camels for the Desert Festival of Jaisalmer, in India. The animals are not merely transport; they also provide milk and meat.

Filling station

Camels can go without drinking for more than a week, but when they reach a well or oasis, they can swallow 110 litres (24 gallons) in 10 minutes!

On your marks...

Camel racing is popular in Australia and Arabia. This traditional sport is now big business, with lots of money spent on preparing for races.

Down under

Nearly half of Australia is desert. The Gibson, Great Sandy, and Great Victoria together form the Outback. All the deserts are home to some very strange-looking animals!

Australia

The mole's tiny eyes are hidden – it uses smell and touch to find its way around.

Coming up for the kill

Marsupial moles live underground, only surfacing if they detect food. Their strong, flat claws are ideal for burrowing – and for killing prey.

Kangaroos are marsupials – they carry their young in a pouch.

A red kangaroo joey spends about 190 days in its mother's pouch. It might return for another 35 days to sleep and feed or if danger threatens.

The very long, strong tail gives a kangaroo stability and power when it hops.

Mob rule

Millions of red kangaroo live all over Australia, in groups (called "mobs") of up to 10 animals. Male kangaroos deliver powerful kicks from their hind legs to show who's boss within the mob.

Honey monsters

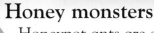

Honeypot ants are so full of food they cannot move. Other ants in the colony bring them food to keep them fat; then, when food is scarce, the colony feeds on the sugar that the "living larders" vomit up.

A spiky character

The short-nosed echidna routs out ants and termites with its snout, then licks them up with its long, sticky tongue. It is a monotreme – a mammal that lays eggs.

Spines provide water as well as defence: the lizard drinks dew that collects on them.

BORN TO BE WILD

The only place where dromedary camels roam free today is Australia. They are descendants of domestic camels that explorers had taken over from the Middle East between 1840 and 1907, to use as transport. By the 1930s they were replaced with cars and left to run wild.

Get the point

Under all those spines is a lizard! The thorny devil needs such protection because the small reptile moves very slowly, seeking insects to eat. It can swallow 2,500 of them in one meal.

Bigger and bolder

Up to seven times bigger than a thorny devil, a sand monitor doesn't need spines. It uses its strong tail as a whip to strike attackers.

Cactus country

The cactus is the plant-world's symbol of the desert. However, you won't find them in every desert – these spiky succulents only grow wild in American deserts, including the Sonoran, Mojave, and Chihuahua.

Gila woodpeckers brave the spines to make nesting holes inside the cacti. When they move out, elf owls move in!

Green giant

Giant saguaro cacti grow in the Sonoran Desert. They can reach 15 m (50 ft) tall and live for more than 200 years. Like all cacti, their stems are covered with spines, which are a kind of adapted leaf.

Spines give defence against animals that try to eat the water-filled cactus.

Cacti facts

● It takes around 75 years for a saguaro to grow an "arm".

● Cacti lose less water through their spines than they would if they had normal leaves.

● Two-thirds of the weight of a giant saguaro is water. That's enough to fill 1,000 baths!

Spiky sunscreen

The "old man cactus" has more than spikes on its stem: it has hairs too, which act as a screen against the strong desert sun. White spines are especially good for reflecting the sunlight.

People use aloe juice in cosmetics and as an ointment for cooling burns.

Full to bursting

A cactus is a giant water tank. The plant draws in water through its roots and stores so much that its stem grows fat. The creases on the stem expand just like a concertina.

Aloe aloe

Succulents are plants that store water in their stem or leaves. Like this aloe, they also have a waxy coating to protect the leaves from the sun and wind.

Prickly pears also grow in Australia. They were brought over 200 years ago.

This fruit tastes sharp!

The big, flat pads of a prickly pear are not leaves, but stems. The pads and fruit are covered in spines – but it's not enough to stop animals eating the plant!

The desert in bloom

All plants need water to survive, but it can be hard to find water in the desert – and to keep from losing it. Desert plants have developed clever ways of finding and storing water in the driest of lands.

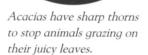

Acacias have sharp thorns to stop animals grazing on their juicy leaves.

Pebble plants blend in with desert gravel, hidden from animals that might eat them.

The root of the matter

Acacia trees provide shade and shelter for many animals in the open desert. The trees can grow in the dry land because they have very long roots that search for moisture deep underground.

The ends of the leaves may dry out and die, but they keep on growing – up to 6 m (20 ft) long!

It takes two

Plants lose water through their leaves, so the best way to keep water is to have few leaves. Welwitschia and pebble plants have just two each, although they could hardly look more different.

Roses of Jericho are also called "resurrection plants".

Back to life

When there is no water, rose of Jericho plants dry up so much they look like they are dead. But a "miracle" occurs when the rains come: the plant comes back to life!

Water storage tanks

The fruit of a desert melon plant is full of stored water, just like the melons you find in shops. Thirsty animals wandering through the desert devour whole patches of these wild plants.

The Sonoran looks empty in the dry season.

Speedy bloomers

The Sonoran Desert becomes a riot of colour after a spring rainfall. Seeds that fell on the dry ground the year before quickly germinate and grow into flowers in just a few weeks.

Who lives there?

Despite the blistering daytime heat, freezing cold nights, and dusty, dry environment, there are people living in every hot desert in the world. Many of them are nomadic: they move around the desert in search of water.

Unlike Bedouins, Aborigines keep cool by not wearing many clothes.

Less is more

Aborigines in the Australian deserts traditionally wore very little. Now they mostly wear modern dress, but will put on loincloths and body paint for ceremonies.

Bedouins wear long, flowing robes and head scarves to keep the sun off them.

Bedouin men play the rabbaba to entertain guests.

Bedouins and Tuaregs used to load their tents and possessions onto camels when moving home. Today, they often use trucks.

Mobile homes

The Bedouins of the Middle East are nomads, so they need houses that are easy to transport and put up. Their rug-lined tents have dark covers made of goat hair, keeping the inside cool and shady.

Houses an

Tuaregs live in the Sahara.

People of the veil

A Tuareg man is easily recognised by his veil, the *tagelmust*. Tuaregs believe that the veil protects against evil spirits. It also shields the face from sand.

Desert dwellings: Permanent...

People living in the Thar Desert are not nomadic. They build solid homes out of local materials: straw, sand, and camel dung.

Temporary...

In the Kalahari, San people shelter in grass huts when the rains come. In the summer they might not build huts at all, just a screen to block out the wind.

Underground!

Whole towns of stone- or brick-built houses can be found in some deserts. In Australia, opal miners carved houses out of cool underground caves.

lothes need to keep people warm at night, but cool during the day.

There isn't much furniture to pack up when moving.

A curtain separates the women's area from the men, giving them privacy.

31

Desert daily life

There are many things that people do every day, such as working, making meals, and playing sport or music. People in the desert do all this too – but probably not in the same way as you!

The arrow is coated with poison that comes from beetle larvae.

Hunting is the main way San find food.

Arts and crafts

Making jewellery is one of many desert crafts. Women work with leather, wool, and beads, while men forge metal into jewellery, saddle decorations, and swords.

Going hunting

It takes a lot of skill to hunt in the desert. San men know how to follow animal tracks to find prey such as antelope. Silently they crouch low, take aim, and kill the animal with their poison arrows.

Aborigines used boomerangs as their hunting weapons, throwing the curved wooden clubs at prey.

The speediest racing camels have long, straight legs and big muscles, but small feet.

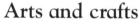

Local races are a way of reviving old traditions as people in the desert become more modern.

Women spin the wool and dye it with bright colours.

A woman's work

While the men are out working, Bedouin women run the home, doing everything from milking the camels and cooking to making clothes and getting firewood.

The wool comes from the family's goats and sheep, or may be bought.

Time to relax

Playing music is a popular pastime in the long, dark desert evenings. Aborigines traditionally play a didgeridoo, a hollow tree branch that is as tall as a child!

Clothes, bags, and rugs are woven from sheep's wool.

Who's the best?

Camels are such a major part of desert people's lives, they are even used for sport. Traditional camel racing gave people the chance to show off how good their camel was.

Food and drink

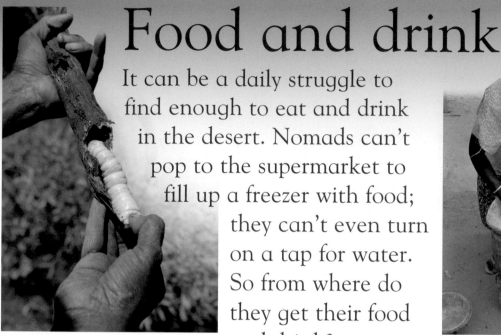

It can be a daily struggle to find enough to eat and drink in the desert. Nomads can't pop to the supermarket to fill up a freezer with food; they can't even turn on a tap for water. So from where do they get their food and drink?

The witchetty grub, a kind of moth larva, is the best known "bush tucker" – food that Aborigines find in the desert.

Millet grain is pounded and made into porridge.

Fresh food

Tuaregs eat what their animals give them: meat, eggs, and dairy products such as milk and yogurt. They sell any extra food to buy millet from local markets.

People decorate their eggshells to show whose is whose.

Egg stores

Water is such a precious resource that it needs to be stored carefully. San people fill empty ostrich eggshells with water, and bury them to keep them cool and safe.

Food for all

Bedouin men share their meals with guests, scooping up rice and meat with their fingers from a large centre plate. Women cook the meal, then go to eat in their own part of the tent.

Plenty of food can fit onto this plate: it can hold a whole cooked sheep!

It is very important to be a generous host: one day you might need a return meal.

Time for tea

Tuaregs show hospitality through their tea ceremony. Green tea leaves, sugar, and water are boiled on an open fire to make a strong brew for the guests.

Bedouins prefer coffee to tea, and serve three small cups to each guest.

It's a man's job to greet guests and perform the tea ceremony.

The pot is poured from high up so the tea is frothy.

Twice as tough

Animals and plants in cold deserts, such as the Gobi and Patagonia, don't just have to cope with hot summers – they also have to survive freezing winters, when the temperature can plummet to -40 °C (-40 °F).

There aren't many plants in the rocky Gobi, but the saxaul grows here in clumps. The woody shrub grows twice as tall as a person.

Leopard geckos search for food at night, storing fat in their tails to get by in extreme weather. In winter, they hibernate.

A coat for all seasons

Bactrian camels have woolly coats to keep warm in the winter, but in the summer the heat can be overbearing. So in the spring, they begin their annual moult.

BACK FROM THE BRINK?

Przewalski horses used to roam the Gobi, but today they are officially extinct in the wild. Luckily, some survived in zoos, and these were used in a breeding programme so the species could be brought back to the Gobi. Now there are around 1,500 horses in Gobi national parks.

Welcome home

It's hard to find food in the snowy Gobi winter.

The hair falls off in thick clumps, leaving a sparse layer for the summer. It will grow back in the autumn.

Changing with the weather

Hairy armadillos change their behaviour with the seasons. In the winter, when it is cold, they are active in the daytime; but in the summer they stay in burrows to avoid the heat, and come out at night instead.

What am I?

The mara looks a bit like a large rabbit or a small deer, but it is actually a rodent, so it is closer to being a huge rat! Maras can run very fast, up to 48 km/h (30 mph), when escaping predators in the open desert.

Even in the summer, strong winds keep the Patagonia Desert bare.

Patagonia, in South America, lies in the shadow of the Andes Mountains. Very few plants can survive the dry weather and strong winds here.

A long walk home

Magellanic penguins live on the coast and feed in the sea. But in the breeding season they waddle 1.6 km (1 mile) inland across the desert dunes, where they dig burrows to lay their eggs in.

Living in the Gobi

Mongolian nomads move around to find pasture for their animals. It's not easy in the extreme Gobi weather – the nomads have to settle before the snow does.

Dried animal dung is collected, piled up, and burnt as fuel.

The nomads wear thick, warm clothes in the winter.

Hunting
Golden eagles are important to the Mongolians. The men train the birds to hunt for foxes and rabbits.

Follow the herd
Mongolians are herders: they keep camels, yaks, sheep, and goats for milk, meat, and wool. Nothing goes to waste – even the dung is used!

Gers in the Gobi
Mongolians live in *gers*, sturdy mobile homes that can keep out the cold weather. The *ger's* wooden frame collapses and fits neatly onto a truck when it's time to move on.

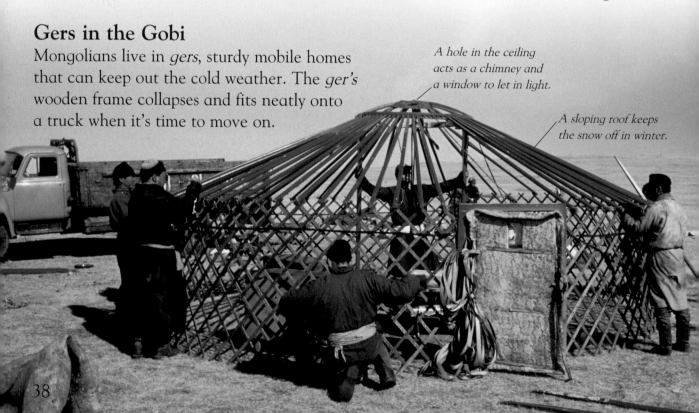

A hole in the ceiling acts as a chimney and a window to let in light.

A sloping roof keeps the snow off in winter.

Starting young

Mongolians are most famous for being horsemen. They have a saying that children are taught to ride before they can walk! Horses are also milked as well as ridden.

Sporting skills

Mongolian men work hard and play hard. Their favourite sport is wrestling. Along with horsemanship and archery, it is one of their "three manly skills".

It's the women's job to milk the animals. Fermented horse milk makes a tasty drink.

Interior design

Inside the home is warm and snug. While the practical *ger* looks plain from the outside, lots of bright colours inside cheer up the bleak landscape.

Not all gers *are entirely traditional – some even have TVs.*

The heavy felt walls are made from sheep's wool. The ropes are yak hair.

It's cool to be coastal

The Atacama Desert in South America runs alongside the Pacific Ocean, yet it is the driest place on Earth. Some parts of the cool desert have not seen rainfall since records began – that's at least 400 years.

WHY IS THE ATACAMA SO DRY?

Even compared to other deserts, the Atacama is extra dry. When the Sun has warmed the air in the desert, no rain falls because warm air holds in water. There is fog from the ocean to the west, but it is quickly burnt off by the Sun. And to the east the Andes mountains block any rainclouds, which leaves the Atacama trapped high and dry in the middle.

Watch this space

The Atacama landscape is so bare, it has been compared to the Moon and Mars – so much so that NASA uses it to test space equipment.

Coastal cacti

The fog that forms over the ocean provides just enough moisture for plants such as cacti to grow along the coast. Further inland, the desert is too dry for any plants to grow at all.

As well as being coastal, the Atacama is high up in the Andes Mountains, where the air is cool.

Cold ocean currents keep the air temperature cool.

The same difference

Although still very dry, the Namib Desert in southwest Africa is different to the Atacama because it is not mountainous. Fog rolls in from the sea over vast sand dunes, bringing water to animals, including fog-basking beetles.

As moisture condenses on the beetle's shell, the insect bends forward to roll the droplet into its mouth to drink.

Camel cousins

Guanacos are the South American relatives of camels. They can wander through the desert for many days without needing to drink.

Flamingo frenzy

There is some water in the Atacama, mostly in salt lakes. These lakes are home to thousands of flamingos, which gather to feed in the shallow waters.

Guanacos pick up moisture through their food as they graze on the Andean slopes.

Is it a desert?

Antarctica, the continent around the South Pole, has very little precipitation (what scientists call rain, snow, and hail). This makes it a desert – and it's the biggest in the world.

Whiteout!

There's no rain at all in the world's coldest, windiest continent – it's so cold, it gets snow instead. Not much actually falls, but strong winds blow the snow about, causing blinding blizzards.

Plentiful penguins

Emperor penguins only come to land to raise their chicks. After laying her egg, the female returns to the sea for food, leaving the male in charge.

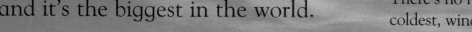

The only large animals in Antarctica

Left on his own, the male doesn't eat while he looks after the egg.

Eight weeks later, the females return with food for their newborn chicks.

Where are all the plants?

Mosses and algae are the only plants in Antarctica. There are no trees or bushes; their roots would not be able to get through the frozen ground.

Like mosses and algae, types of fungus called lichen grow on rocks in the Antarctic.

The wrong name?

What do crabeater seals eat mostly? Not crabs, but krill! As they swim in the sea, they lock their teeth together into a "sieve" to collect the food from the water.

Krill are shrimp-like animals.

live in the sea. There's not enough food for them to live on land.

What about the Arctic?

The area around the North Pole, where polar bears live, is an icecap on top of the sea. Although the Arctic has no rain, it also has no land, so it can't be called a desert.

43

The growing desert

The amount of desert in the world is getting larger. Rivers are drying up, grasslands are disappearing, and more and more land is turning bare. There are two main reasons for desertification: nature and human beings.

Do your bit!

Global warming is a major cause of desertification: as the world gets warmer, the land dries out. Everybody should do their bit to save energy and help slow down global warming. This can be as simple as turning off the light when you leave a room!

Do you use energy-saving light bulbs and recycled paper?

What's the problem?

It's thought that 250 million people will be affected by desertification. The growing desert will bury homes and make it hard to find food, and dust storms will reach big cities more often, triggering diseases such as asthma.

Desertification facts

Most scientists agree that the main reason that deserts are spreading is land misuse. This includes:

- chopping down trees
- clearing land for farming
- over-grazing animals

More than a quarter of land on Earth is at risk of desertification.

Sahel survivors

Ostriches can be found in the Sahel, the semi-desert south of the Sahara. Not many other animals can survive there; they move away or die out as the Sahel's desert conditions get worse.

Flightless ostriches walk long distances to find grass and other plants to eat.

The grass holds down the sand, stopping it from blowing away.

Sand fences

One way to stop the desert spreading is to plant trees to hold back the sand. In China, people have planted grass in the Gobi to try to stop the sand and dust storms reaching the cities so often.

The crops are watered by a pipe that turns in the middle of the circle.

Crop circles

These huge green circles found in American, African, and Middle Eastern deserts are fields! Irrigating, or watering, the land allows farmers to grow crops such as wheat and tomatoes.

Goats have been introduced to many deserts in Africa and India.

Greedy goats

People in the desert keep goats because they provide wool, milk, and meat. But goats are not good for the desert – they eat everything, stripping the land of plants. The bare soil gets blown away, leaving just sand behind.

Glossary

Here are the meanings of some words
it is useful to know when learning about deserts.

Arachnid animals that have eight legs and bodies divided into two sections, such as spiders and scorpions.

Arid when something is arid, it is very dry. Arid land has very little water.

Barren something that is empty of life. Barren land cannot support plants.

Camouflage a colour or pattern that blends in with its surroundings, so it can't be seen.

Cold-blooded animals that warm up or cool down depending on the temperature around them. Reptiles are cold-blooded.

Desert an area that gets less than 25 cm (10 in) of rainfall in a year. In a desert, more water evaporates than falls.

Desertification the spread of desert-like conditions.

Diurnal animals that are diurnal are active during the day.

Dune a hill of sand that has been blown into shape by the wind.

Dust storm strong winds that pick up sand and dust. Dust can be blown thousands of kilometres (miles).

Fertile when an animal or plant can reproduce, it is fertile. Ground that is fertile is good for growing plants.

Global warming the rise in Earth's temperature. It affects the world's weather, causing droughts and severe storms.

Irrigation watering the land using man-made methods such as pipes or canals. Desert farmers use irrigation to water their crops.

Mammal animals that produce milk to feed their young, such as camels, cats, and humans.

Marsupial mammals whose females carry their young in a pouch, such as kangaroos.

Nocturnal animals that are nocturnal are active during the night.

Nomad a person that regularly moves from place to place, taking their home with them.

Oasis a fertile area within a desert. Oases usually have a pool of water surrounded by trees. Animals come to drink the water.

Pinnacle the remains of a mountain or large rock that has been worn away by the wind. They are often needle-shaped.

Predator an animal that hunts, kills, and eats other animals.

Prey the animal that is hunted, killed, and eaten by a predator.

Reptile animals that have tough, scaly skin, such as lizards and snakes. Most lay eggs rather than give birth to live young.

Rodent mammals that have strong front teeth for gnawing, such as jerboas.

Succulent plants that store water in their leaves or stem, such as cacti.

Venom a poisonous liquid. Snakes and scorpions have venom; they bite or sting to inject the venom as defence or for killing prey.

Warm-blooded the opposite of "cold-blooded". Animals and birds that can keep their body temperatures on a constant level. Mammals are warm-blooded.

Index

Aborigine 30, 32, 33, 34
aloe 27
Antarctica 6-7, 42-43
ants 25
Arctic 43
armadillo 37
Atacama Desert 4-5, 6, 40-41
Australian deserts 7, 21, 23, 24-25, 30, 31

Bedouin 30-31, 33, 35
beetle 41

cactus 4-5, 26-27, 40
camel 5, 10, 15, 17, 20, 22-23, 25, 31, 36, 38
camel racing 23, 32-33
coastal deserts 5, 6-7, 40-41
cold deserts 6-7, 36-37, 38-39

desert melon 29
desert rose 8
desertification 44-45
dunes 4, 9, 14
dung 31, 38
dust storm 10-11

eagle 38
echidna 25
Elephant Rock 8

fennec fox 19
flamingo 41
fog 40-41
food 16, 17, 18, 20, 23, 25, 32, 34-35, 36, 41, 42, 43

gemsbok 13
global warming 44
goat 33, 38, 45
Gobi Desert 7, 11, 22, 36, 38-39
gravel 4, 14
guanaco 41

hot deserts 5, 6-7, 14-15, 16-17, 18-19, 30-31
house 30-31, 38-39
hunting 18-19, 20-21, 32, 38

jerboa 19

Kalahari Desert 31
kangaroo 17, 24

lizards 15, 16, 17, 19, 20, 25, 36
locust 15

mara 37
marsupial mole 24
Mongolians 38-39
mountain 8
    Andes 37, 40
music 30, 33

Namib Desert 7, 41
NASA 40

oasis 4, 12-13, 23
ostrich 44
owl 8, 27

Patagonia Desert 6, 37
pebble plant 28
penguin 37, 42-43
people 5, 10, 13, 22, 23, 30-31, 32-33, 34-35, 38-39, 44, 45
pinnacle 8
plants 4-5, 12, 15, 26-27, 28-29, 36, 40, 43

rain 4, 12, 40, 42, 43
river 4, 13, 44
rock 4, 8, 14
rose of Jericho 29

Sahara 4-5, 7, 11, 13, 14-15, 22, 31, 44
Sahel 44
San 31, 32, 34
sand 4, 8-9, 10, 11, 14, 23
sand cat 18
sandgrouse 12
scorpion 19, 20
snakes 17, 18, 21
snow 36, 38-39, 42
Sonoran Desert 4-5, 6, 26, 29
springbok 16

tarantula 20
tent 30-31, 38-39
Thar Desert 7, 13, 31
toad 16
tree 12, 28, 36, 43
Tuareg 31, 34, 35

venom 19, 20-21

water 8, 12-13, 16, 17, 26, 27, 28, 29, 30, 34, 40, 41, 45
welwitschia 28
wind 8, 9, 11
wrestling 39

Acknowledgements

Dorling Kindersley would like to thank:
Andy Cooke for artwork; Simon Mumford for cartography.

Picture credits

The publisher would like to thank the following for their kind permission to reproduce their photographs:
(a=above; c=centre; b=below; l=left; r=right; t=top)
Alamy Images: Arco Images 39cl, 39tl; Around the World in a Viewfinder 32tr; Suzy Bennett 34tl; Blickwinkel 12-13bc, 19tc, 24cr; Danita Delimont 38tl; Dinodia Images 23tr; Elvele Images/CGE 42bl, 43br; Robert Estall Photo Agency 31tl; Mark Eveleigh 25bc; Pavel Filatov 39crb; Glen Islet 27tr; Israel images 6bl; Andrea Jones 27tl; Juniors Bildarchiv 46bl; Wolfgang Kaehler 39tr; Tomas Kaspar 8br; David Kilpatrick 12ca; Emmanuel Lattes 27br; Lou Linwei 11tl; LOOK Die Bildagentur der Fotografen GmbH 1c, 15br; Alex Maddox 25cra; Ellen McKnight 3br; Bernd Mellmann 14-15b; nagelestock.com 30t; Joe Nebrasz 43tr; Peter Richard Noble 31tr; Dale O'Dell 4-5c; Gerry Pearce 25tl; Peter Adams Photography 39bc; Picpics 8tr; Robert Preston 13br; Robert Harding Picture Library 23br, 35tr; Slick Shoots 46-47cb; Simon Stirrup 28tr; Stockfolio 22cl; David Tipling 43tl; Tribaleye Images/Jamie Marshall 4-5b; David Wall 31crb; Marcus Wilson-Smith 7tr; **Ardea:** John Cancalosi 2tl, 16cra; Jean-Paul Ferrero 24bc;

Mike W Gillam 24tr; François Grohier 37tl, 37tr; **John Conley:** John Conley 40tr; **Corbis:** Theo Allofs/Zefa 41b; Yann Arthus-Bertrand 14tr, 45cl, 45r; Craig Aurness 10bl, 10-11bc; Jonathan Blair 13tr; Fridmar Damm 2-3; Eyal Ofer 32-33b; Michael & Patricia Fogden 21tl; Gallo Images 6br, 34bl; George H H Huey 29c; Peter Johnson 28bc, 32cla, 32tl, 34br; Frans Lemmens 15tr, 48; David Muench 26c; Kazuyoshi Nomachi 8cl; Reuters 44tl, 45tl; Galen Rowell 42tr; Scott T. Smith 29crb; Sygma/Patrick Robert 15cr; Penny Tweedie 25tr; Steffan Widstrand 28ca; Alison Wright 13clb; **Eye Ubiquitous:** Hutchison 31cra; **FLPA:** Jim Brandenburg/Minden 41tl; Flip de Nooyer/Foto Natura 37b; Michael & Patricia Fogden 16bc, 41cl; Tom and Pam Gardner 17tl; Chris Mattison 21tr; Mark Moffett/Minden 20cra; Norbert Wu/Minden 42-43c; **Getty Images:** Robert Harding World Imagery 30bl; G K & Vicky Hart 22c; Michael Melford 11tr; George H. H. Huey Photography: 27bl; **Impact Photos:** 30-31b; **Lonely Planet Images:** Graham Taylor 38bc; **Magnum Photos:** Steve McCurry 10tr; **naturepl.com:** Graham Hatherley 19cr; Tom Mangelsen 18tr; Vincent Munier 44b; Gabriel Rojo 41cr; **OSF:** 36br; John Brown 40b; Michael Fogden 17cr; Travel Library Ltd 4-5t; Ariadne van Zandbergen 35b; **Photolibrary:** Workbook Inc. 36tr; **Photoshot/NHPA:** Martin Harvey 29tr; Daniel Heuclin 17bl, 19bc, 19tl, 21b, 29tl; **PunchStock:** Goodshot 23cr; **Science Photo Library:** G K Lorenx 26ca; **stevebloom.com:** 7br; **Still Pictures:** 34tr; Joffe Dragesco 18cb; Raimund Franken 33tl; Thomas Haertrich 8-9; Hartmut Schwarzbach 30cr; **SuperStock:** age fotostock 15tl, 36bl; **Dr Olga Pereladova/WWF International:** 36tl

All other images © Dorling Kindersley.
For further information see www.dkimages.com